BRIGHT IDEA BOOKS

YOU CAN WORK IN Theatre

by Samantha S. Bell

raintree
a Capstone company — publishers for children

Raintree is an imprint of Capstone Global Library Limited, a company incorporated in England and Wales having its registered office at 264 Banbury Road, Oxford, OX2 7DY – Registered company number: 6695582

www.raintree.co.uk
myorders@raintree.co.uk

Edited by Charly Haley
Designed by Becky Daum
Production by Claire Vanden Branden
Originated by Capstone Global Library Ltd
Printed and bound in India

ISBN 978 1 4747 7533 5 (hardback)
22 21 20 19 18
10 9 8 7 6 5 4 3 2 1

ISBN 978 1 4747 7357 7 (paperback)
22 21 20 19 18
10 9 8 7 6 5 4 3 2 1

British Library Cataloguing in Publication Data
A full catalogue record for this book is available from the British Library.

Acknowledgements
We would like to thank the following for permission to reproduce photographs: iStockphoto: ferrantraite, 15, Steve Debenport, 26-27; Shutterstock Images: A_Lesik, 20-21, Andrey Petrovas, cover (foreground), 29, Chris Cornish, 24-25, Christian Bertrand, 16-17, Dean Drobot, 6-7, dibrova, 8-9, Igor Bulgarin, 19, 30-31, Kozlik, cover (background), 11, 23, Pavel L Photo and Video, 5, Rommel Canlas, 12. Design Elements: iStockphoto, Red Line Editorial, and Shutterstock Images.

3 8002 02422 508 0

CONTENTS

CHAPTER ONE
PRODUCERS 4
CHAPTER TWO
CAST MEMBERS 10
CHAPTER THREE
DIRECTORS 14
CHAPTER FOUR
MUSIC DIRECTORS 18
CHAPTER FIVE
STAGE MANAGERS 22

Glossary 28
Find out more 29
Activity 30
Index.................................... 32

CHAPTER 1

PRODUCERS

An actor speaks onstage. Other actors join him. They sing and dance. They wear costumes. It's a West End show!

The West End is a famous area of London. There are many theatres in that area. West End theatres are among the best in the world. Some West End plays are **musicals**.

Many different people work in theatre. It takes a lot of people to put on a show. They all work together. They want to make the show the best it can be.

Plays and musicals often have many actors.

It all starts with the **producer**. Producers read play **scripts**. They choose a play. They get the money to put on the show.

The producer chooses the **director**. They work together. They work with the music director too.

People who write scripts want producers to read their work. They want producers to make their scripts into plays.

Theatre shows are often advertised on huge screens in busy areas.

Producers also **advertise** their plays. They tell people to watch shows at the theatre.

Producers need to be good leaders. They must work well with other people. They may have studied writing or acting.

CHAPTER 2

CAST Members

The people who are in a play are called cast members. They can be actors and singers. They may be dancers. Most must **audition** for their **roles**.

Actors spend hours onstage during a show. They may have a lot of **lines**.

HAIR AND MAKE-UP ARTISTS

Hair and make-up artists are important too. They make actors look like the characters in the play.

Actors wear costumes when they perform.

Cast members practise the show many times. They must get ready to perform in front of people. This is called **rehearsing**.

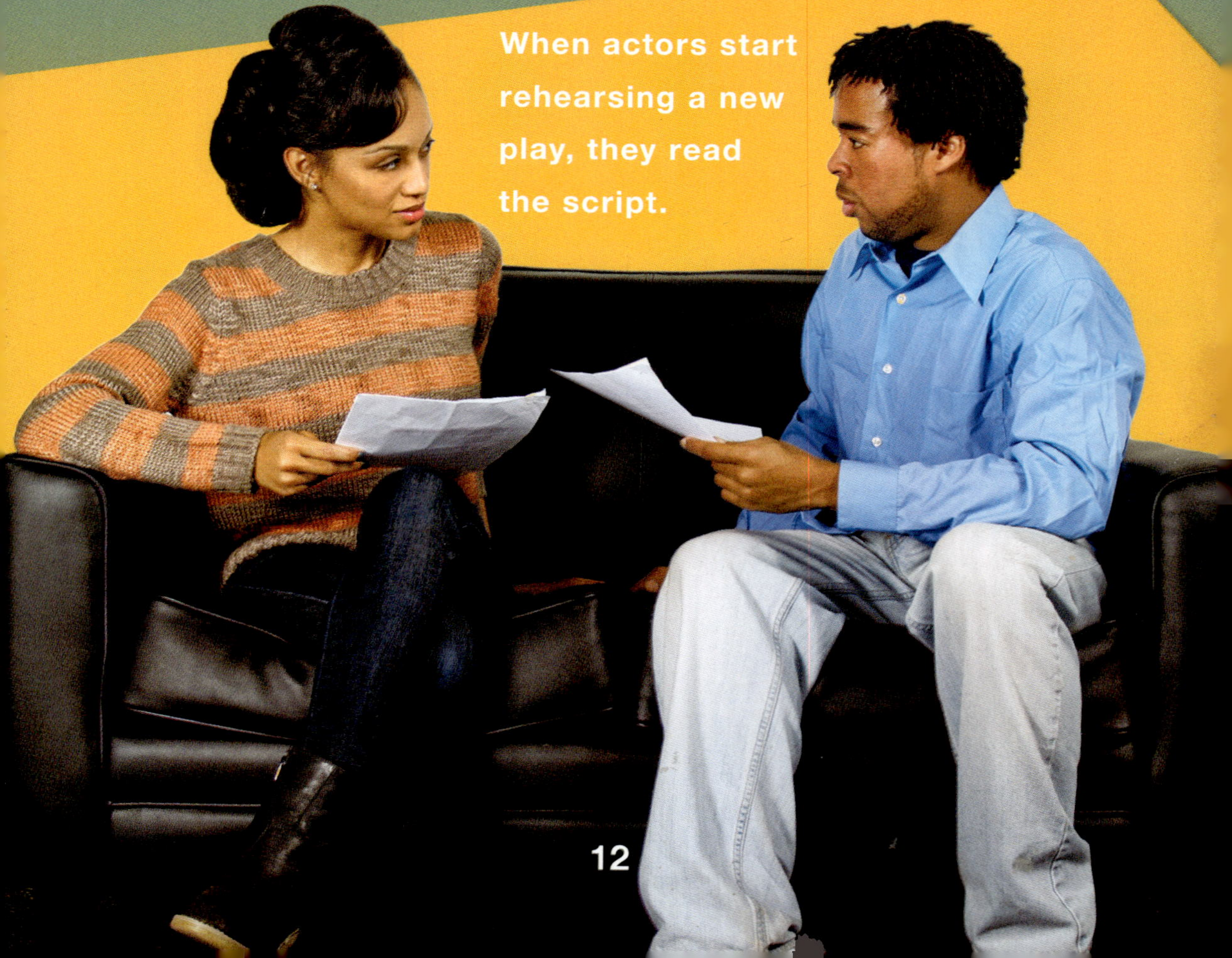

When actors start rehearsing a new play, they read the script.

Cast members may get nervous before a show. But they learn to stay calm. They perform with a lot of energy. They may do eight shows in one week!

Some actors go to university to learn about acting and the theatre. Some begin by acting in school plays. Others act in small theatres.

CHAPTER 3

DIRECTORS

Directors guide everyone who works on a play. Directors help show the story on the stage. They want people to understand the story.

Directors make sure everyone works together.

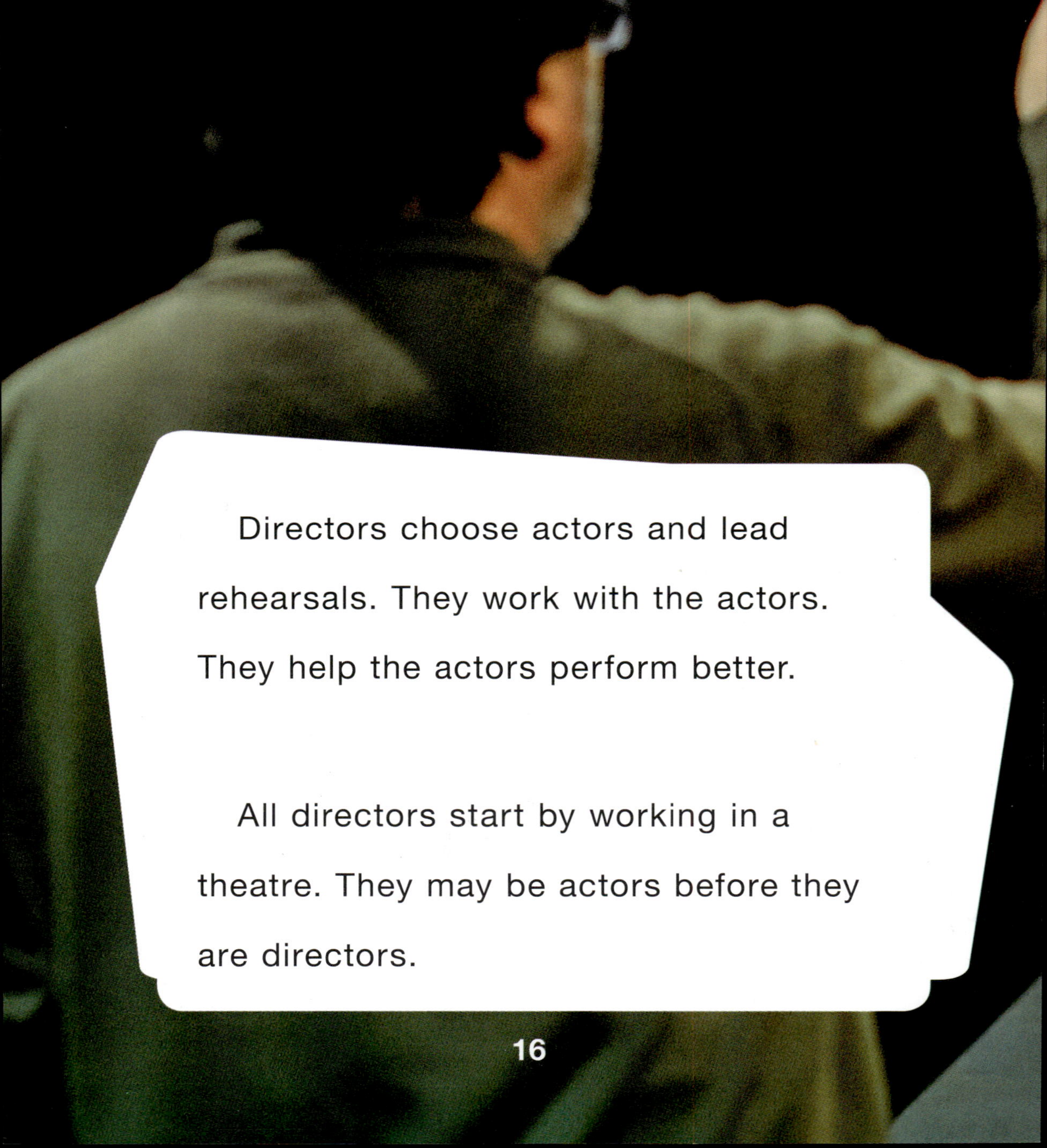

Directors choose actors and lead rehearsals. They work with the actors. They help the actors perform better.

All directors start by working in a theatre. They may be actors before they are directors.

A director sometimes works with one actor at a time.

CHAPTER 4

MUSIC Directors

Music directors organize the music for plays and shows. They help the musicians and actors learn songs.

CHOREOGRAPHERS

Choreographers create dances for the show. They listen to the music and songs. They think about the story. They want the dances to look good.

In musicals, actors sing and dance to music.

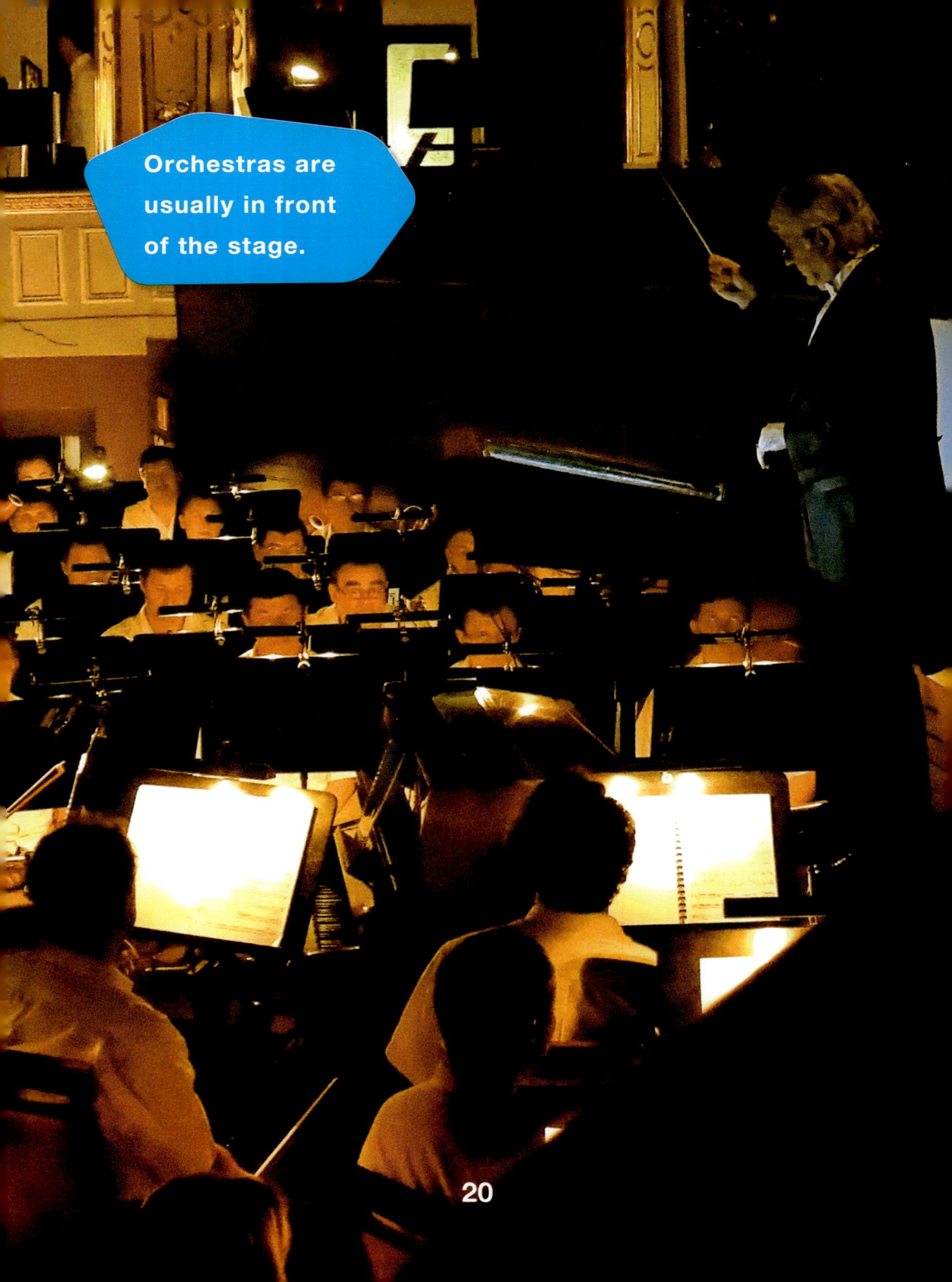

Orchestras are usually in front of the stage.

Most plays have an **orchestra**. The orchestra has many musicians. They play music for the show.

The music director **conducts** the show. This helps all musicians know when to play. It helps them sound good together.

Some music directors have been to university. They often start by working as musicians.

CHAPTER 5

STAGE Managers

Stage **managers** make sure the show runs smoothly. Most stage managers are part of a team. They take turns doing many jobs.

Stage managers plan rehearsals. They keep track of costumes and **props**.

COSTUME AND SET DESIGNERS

Costume designers choose what actors wear. They make actors look like their characters. Set designers make the play's setting on the stage. They might build a fake house for the actors.

Sets, props and costumes help a play come to life.

Stage managers work with stagehands. Stagehands are people who work **backstage**. They move the sets and get props.

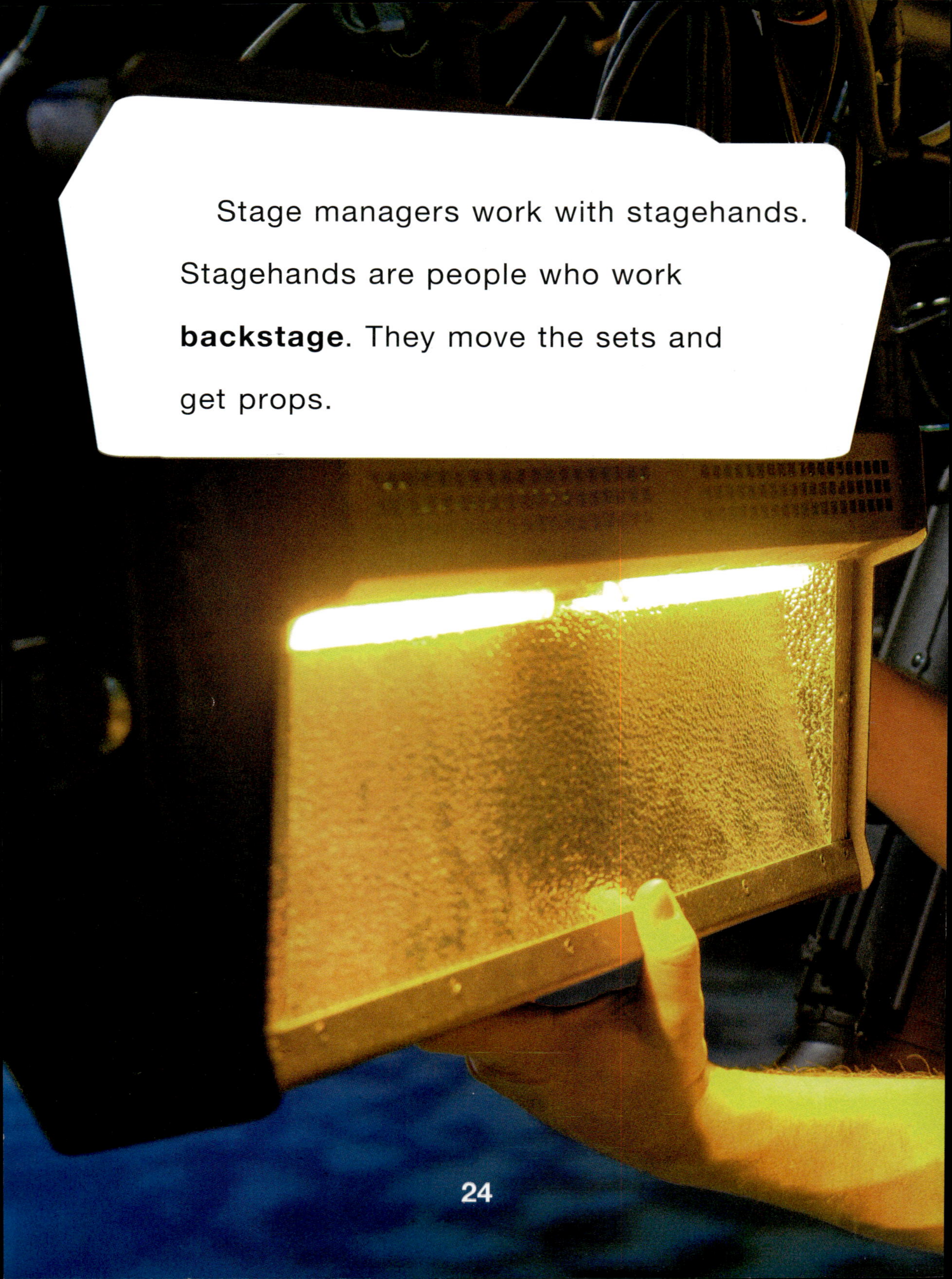

People backstage run lights and sound for plays.

Do you dream of performing onstage or working backstage? You might like to work in theatre!

Stage managers give **cues** during shows. A cue might tell an actor when to go onstage. There are also cues for lights and sound. Most shows have hundreds of cues.

Stage managers deal with problems during a show. They make sure everything works well. They help if an actor is hurt.

Most stage managers have worked backstage first. Later they become managers.

GLOSSARY

advertise
tell people about something that is being sold

audition
short performance given by a performer to see if they are good enough to be in a play

backstage
behind the stage of a theatre

choreographer
person who makes dance routines

conduct
direct singers or musicians

cue
signal for someone to do something

director
person who is in charge of actors and crew members

lines
parts of the script that the actors say out loud

manager
person who is in charge of a project or organization

musical
play that tells a story with songs

orchestra
group of musicians who play different instruments

producer
person who manages money and other parts of making a play

prop
object used by actors in a show

rehearse
practise a play

role
character played by an actor

script
written form of a play, including lines for actors

FIND OUT MORE

Do you want to learn more about the theatre? Check out these resources:

Books

Musical Theatre (Starstruck), Cathy West (Ransom Publishing, 2011)

National Theatre: All About Theatre (Walker Books, 2015)

Website

www.dkfindout.com/uk/music-art-and-literature/shakespeares-globe
Find out about theatre in the time of William Shakespeare.

Place to visit

The Victoria and Albert Museum, London
www.vam.ac.uk/page/t/theatre-and-performance-galleries
This museum has an area that focuses on theatre and performance.

ACTIVITY

PUT ON A SHOW!

Ask a parent or teacher to help you find songs from a musical online. Choose your favourite one and learn the words. Next, decide if you will add dancing. Listen to the music. Create a dance. Decide what costume you will wear. Finally, call your family or friends together to watch your show!

INDEX

acting 4, 9, 10–13, 16, 18, 23, 26–27
advertising 9

backstage 24, 27

costumes 4, 22, 23

dancing 4, 10, 19
directors 6, 14–16

hair and make-up artists 11

London 4

music directors 6, 18–21
musicals 4, 5, 19

orchestras 21

producers 6–9
props 22, 24

rehearsing 12, 16, 22

scripts 6
set designers 23
singing 4, 10
stage managers 22–27
stagehands 24

theatres 4–5, 9, 13

university 9, 13, 16, 21, 27